D0323836

The Gift of Grandparenting

*The best place to be when you're
sad is a grandparent's lap*

PROVERB

The Gift of
Grandparenting

Sharing the delights of being a grandparent

Cheryl Saban PhD

*A treasure trove of stories and memories
about people we hold most dear.*

RYLAND PETERS & SMALL
LONDON • NEW YORK

In loving memory of grandmothers and grandfathers, past and present.

DESIGNER Barbara Zuñiga
COMMISSIONING EDITOR Annabel Morgan
PICTURE RESEARCH Christina Borsi
HEAD OF PRODUCTION Patricia Harrington
ART DIRECTOR Leslie Harrington
EDITORIAL DIRECTOR Julia Charles

First published in 2014 by
Ryland Peters & Small
20–21 Jockey's Fields
London WC1R 4BW
and
519 Broadway, Fifth Floor
New York, NY 10012
www.rylandpeters.com

Text copyright © Cheryl Saban 2014

Design and photography copyright
© Ryland Peters & Small 2014, except images
credited otherwise on page 62.

10 9 8 7 6 5 4 3 2 1

All rights reserved. No part of this publication
may be reproduced, stored in a retrieval system, or
transmitted in any form or by any means, electronic,
mechanical, photocopying, or otherwise, without the
prior permission of the pulisher.

ISBN 978-1-84975-512-2

Printed and bound in China.

Contents

Introduction

People have said that becoming a grandparent brought them a level of joy that they never thought possible. Perhaps this is similar to the way that parenthood rocks your world. Grandparenthood brings yet another dimension of unconditional love that, once again, changes everything. And it's funny—like parenthood, until you've been there it's a feeling that's difficult to explain.

Grandparents have the best of both worlds. We've already been parents and lived through what worked and what didn't. Now we have a chance to see our offspring take on that responsibility—and we can participate in the fun side of it! Our grandchildren have us all wrapped around their little fingers, and we wouldn't have it any other way. And as grandparents, we have something of tremendous value to give our grandchildren— a great capacity for love, curiosity, patience, and affection.

The pages of this little book contain a celebration of grandparents past and present. Some comments are from grandchildren, others are from the parents in between, and some reflections are from the grandparents themselves. There are at least three generations represented in this love-fest. The thread that connects all the stories is the love, appreciation, and admiration that flows between the generations—the special connections formed, the advice given and heeded, and the memories created.

Once upon a time, stories like these were told to each generation in turn to ensure that a family's history survived. And as you read these reflections, perhaps some of them will resonate and remind you of times you've shared with your grandparents.

Perfect love sometimes does not come until the first grandchild.

WELSH PROVERB

Blessed is the influence of one true,
loving human soul on another

GEORGE ELIOT

Memory Makers

Grandparents come in all shapes and sizes. They could be youthful, athletic skiers, or they might be ageing and frail. Some wear sturdy orthopedic shoes and loose-fitting clothes, others are slim, trim, and dressed in the latest fashions. While some are great bakers, others call for take-out. It doesn't matter. To our grandchildren, we are *all* interesting and special in our own quirky ways.

As grandparents, we make a lasting impression on our grandchildren. We are ready with open arms for hugs, a wink, and whatever advice they might need. And, what's more, they know that we're interested in every single thing about them. We'll listen to their stories time after time. We'll take each drawing and papier-mâché creation they make for us and give it pride of place in our home. We give our time to them, because we know how very precious that time is.

Grandparents are a stabilizing part of the family circle, because they have proven with the test of time that challenges can be met, goals can be accomplished, and they are still here to tell the tale. And grandparents are memory-makers, because they not only have plenty to share with us from their lives, but also they inspire us to make rich memories of our own. It's up to us to keep the story going.

"My grandmother was one of those women who baked biscuits from scratch every day of her life. And mostly, she grew everything that got eaten in her house in her garden. She was not big on sweets. Except for a curious tower of Coca-Cola, seven crates high, that was piled on the back porch. I don't remember anybody ever drinking them, or even mentioning them, but everybody knew they were there because in the late afternoon the setting sun shone through the necks of their green glass bottles like church windows.

It was years later that I thought to ask my mother about those cokes. Who drank those cokes? 'Oh, those were for you grandkids,' she said. And I checked that night with my cousins—nobody ever knew. I'm a lot like my grandmother, I tend to have something going on every burner, morning to night. And so the memory of those glowing bottles is a valuable lesson: If you buy a tower of Coca-Cola for someone, don't forget to say, 'Honey, there's cokes on the back porch. They're for you.'" — *Randee*

Children begin by loving their parents; as they grow older they judge them; sometimes they forgive them

OSCAR WILDE

Spend quality time with each other.

Grandchildren, seek out special time with your grandparents, and grandparents, spend one-on-one time with your grandchildren. Yours is a unique relationship, worth nurturing.

"I began my fashion career when I was 10, because I was inspired by my beautiful grandmother, Birdye. She would often take me with her to a department store to go shopping, and I would have the best time putting together outfits for her. My grandmother loved clothes and shoes, and I did too. When I was 12, my Grandmother told me that I could keep helping her select outfits, but only if I treated it like a real job. She told me she would pay me $25 an hour, which was a lot of money in those days. She asked me to keep a record of my hours, and to send her an invoice. I was lucky to have such an amazing mentor." — *Catherine*

Being deeply loved by someone gives you strength,
while loving someone deeply gives you courage

LAO TZU

"My grandmother is the most loving person I have ever met. She recently had a minor heart attack and when I called her she wouldn't give me the time of day to ask how she was doing. Instead, she talked to me for 20 minutes about my schoolwork and my athletic awards. My grandfather was not much different. He would tell me stories about his days in World War II and quiz me—not on the facts of his story, but on the life lessons he had learned. He always said smart people learn from their mistakes, but geniuses learn from others' mistakes as well as their own. Unfortunately, he passed away a few years ago, but I will never forget him or his immeasurable love for me." — *Zev*

"I have befriended a grandfather who reminds me of a retired ship's captain with a lifetime of great stories. I love his smile and his strong handshake!" — *Tom*

I can no other answer make but thanks, and thanks; and ever thanks

WILLIAM SHAKESPEARE

"As a little girl, going to my grandparents' ranch was an adventure. There was land to run around on, trees to climb, and an old swing to fight over. My Granny and Grandpa owned a horse, a cow, geese, and chickens. Granny raised the chickens and sold the eggs for her 'egg money,' which was hers to keep. She told us a woman should always have her *own* money.

Although at the time I thought my grandparents were old-fashioned, my grandmother knew what kind of things would make a teenaged girl happy, because she was the one who gave me my very first pair of nylon stockings. I'll never forget how excited I was to open that little package on Christmas Day. A sly look passed between Granny and my Grandpa, and they both grinned. It was as if they knew that my life was going to change in the next few years, and they wanted to be a part of it.

As I look back, I am grateful for all the things my grandparents gave me, just by being themselves. My Granny taught me a love of canning, she taught me how to crochet, she taught me that it's important for women to have their own money, and she taught me that, even when you get older, women like a new pair of sexy stockings now and then." — *Chloe*

"My grandmother and I spent hours in the kitchen—I can still remember the rooster pattern on the wallpaper of her farm. The kitchen was her place—it was the control center of the farm and every major decision made happened in that kitchen. My grandmother, ladle in hand, took care of all of us. My brother came to her kitchen as a child with a skinned knee and as an adult to discuss his job loss. Everything was sorted out by Grandma—everything was discussed while food and drink was served. Solutions were always found." — *Doug*

Ask your grandparents to tell you their stories.

Their lives are rich with details of a world gone by that we can see
only through their eyes.

"I will never forget that my grandfather would give me a big bear hug and say, 'Love and strength are the center of all things. Love and strength do not come from what you say, they are revealed by what you do. Do things well, with abundant love and strength always.' " — *Jason*

"It was the end of my birthday dinner at our favorite sushi place. I was standing with my son, Micha, and my grandson, Max, and had one of those moments in which I felt that certain connection, as three generations of us looked at each other and smiled before saying goodbye for the night. Love…generations…crossing the time barrier and infusing the little space with emotions. Then, Max, aged 8, looked up at us both and said, "You know Daddy, if it weren't for Grandma Sue, you wouldn't be here, and neither would I!" — *Sue*

*The greatest happiness of life is the conviction that
we are loved; loved for ourselves, or rather, loved
in spite of ourselves.*

VICTOR HUGO

"When my daughter told me she was pregnant, the glow of happiness on her eager face could barely compete with the emotional upheaval going on inside me. It was a mixture of thrill, pride, glee, worry, and a rush of overwhelming love. I had become a mother at a young age, and now I'd be a young grandmother too. I was overjoyed. My baby was having a baby!

As the months passed and I watched my daughter's body change and grow, I felt my heart expand right along with her belly. My daughter set her course for first-time parenthood, and I set my course as a grandparent-to-be. As the mother of four, I was able to answer many questions, and provide lots of suggestions, but I was also willing to stand aside and watch her do her thing—which is pretty much what she did.

After the birth, my husband and I joined the new family in the birthing room and met our granddaughter for the first time. I will never forget that moment. The tiny infant, angelic and calm in the arms of my daughter, looked so perfect and tender. I thought of my own mother, now a great-grandmother, and me—now a grandmother. My daughter looked up at me with a dazzling smile and tears shining in her eyes and said, 'Isn't she beautiful, Mama?' Now I know how you and Gramma feel." — *Carolyn*

When the wisdom of the Grandmothers
is heard, the world will heal

HOPI PROPHECY

❋❋❋❋❋❋❋❋❋❋❋

History Lessons

As a little girl, I was lucky to have known both my paternal grandparents, and my mom's mother, my Nana, was a big part of my life until my late teens, as well. There were uncles and aunts, great uncles, great aunts and cousins, but our grandparents held a special stature. As children, we all picked up on that.

Grandparents are the focal point. They bring us together, they are the keepers of traditions and the family core. Even when they have passed away, memories of our beloved grandparents become the folklore of our families. They are the stars of many of the stories we tell our kids to assure them that life goes on, even when times get tough.

Whether you still have the joy of your grandparents in your life or are lucky enough to be a grandparent yourself, you know how sweet and special the connection can be. I remember fondly the family gatherings, the bottomless cookie jar and the laughter lines around my grandparents' eyes. Though money was scarce, they managed to carve out a life for themselves, and they did so without complaint. While material things were in short supply, my grandparents never ran out of common sense or love. As you reflect on your grandparents, consider the lessons you've learned from family and the multi-generational love that surrounds you. In one way or another, I'll bet these lessons made you stronger.

Call your grandparents on the phone from time to time...

...for no reason other than to just say hi...to stay in touch. It's nice to be included. Your gesture will fill their hearts with joy—and yours too.

"My grandma can clean up faster than anyone I have ever seen. She is the tornado of clean. My grandma is sweet. She always smiles and she is always right. My grandma always looks beautiful—she has never changed since the first time she hugged me. Grandmas love you no matter what. Grandmas love you even when you try to tell a joke and it doesn't make sense. Grandmas lovingly teach you all the important things in life, because they have giant hearts. When I wake up at Grandma's house and smell Grandma's cooking, it's the best smell in the world, and she is the best cook in the world. My grandma knows everything. I mean everything. She knows what to do if you lose your school books, she knows what to say if your best friend hurt your feelings, she knows where to find your phone when you lose it…how does she do that?! My Grandma is good with money. She gives it to me. Grandmas are like music—they make you feel good." — *Noah*

My grandson was visiting one day when he asked,
"Gramma, do you know how you and God are alike?"
I mentally polished my halo while I asked, 'No, how are
we alike?' 'You're both old,' he replied.

AUTHOR UNKNOWN

Talk not of wasted affection—affection never was wasted

HENRY WADSWORTH LONGFELLOW

" 'Kindness—the one thing I've never regretted in my life is being kind,' said my grandfather as we sat on his deck in the final months of his struggle with a brain tumor. It would be the last real conversation that we ever had. A psychiatrist who spent his career serving the poor, my grandfather had lived his values and sought to transmit them to me in that final chat about his past and my future. He showed us what it meant to be truly kind through the power of his example: his weekly visits to the county jail, the late-night phone calls with his patients who were having trouble, the "history lessons" he gave his grandchildren on our extended trips through the backwaters of Asia, the relatives struggling with mental illness who lived months and years in his home…and got better. I knew instinctively what he meant when he said at the end of our conversation, 'Nate, there is no one right path for you in life—you will have many opportunities. All I can tell you for sure is that you will never regret being kind.' It's something that I've never forgotten." — *Nathan*

A house needs a grandma in it

LOUISA MAY ALCOTT

"My grandmother was more than my teacher, she was wise like a saint. When I had a bad day, or when something didn't go as I wished, she would tell me, 'If it didn't happen today, it was not meant to happen. Whatever you are supposed to do, and whenever you are supposed to do it, will be revealed to you another day. Things will turn out and you will take appropriate action because you are brave—and, even if you feel scared, know that I love you and you are good enough.' "— *Lois*

If becoming a grandmother was only a matter of choice,
I should advise every one of you straight away to become
one. There is no fun for old people like it!

HANNAH WHITHALL SMITH

"My Grandfather was the family judge and arbiter—not just for my family, for our community as well. He would wisely tell each of us, 'Rather than be angry at the people who may have hurt you, forgive them—and when you have hurt someone else, say you're sorry, or make amends to the people you have hurt—and don't wait for a special occasion to make your apologies. This way,' he explained, 'You can stop the river of hate from flowing.' " — *Benjamin*

"Our grandmother raised 10 of us. I remember how she taught us how to share, no matter how little she had, and to appreciate what we have. She taught us how to bake, cook and wash." — *Eleanor*

I like not only to be loved, but also to be told I am loved.

GEORGE ELIOT

"Our son was 25 when he married and we waited over five years to be given the momentous words, 'You're going to be grandparents!' The day the first bundle of joy was born still lives vividly in my mind. My husband unexpectedly arrived at my office to take me to lunch. Just as we were walking out the front door, the receptionist said there was a long-distance call from New York. It was our son...and we were grandparents of a beautiful baby girl named Amanda! Needless to say, that was a very special and joyous day. Life moved on and we were able to experience this same miracle two more times with the arrivals of Lauren and Jennifer. The opportunity to participate in their lives has been a journey of love and laughter. As we grew older, we experienced the awesome results of their parents' teaching and, hopefully, our influence on their lives. These wonderful granddaughters grew into young women full of courage, integrity and a great capacity to love and express love. Watching this unfold over the years has been a privilege and has given us great joy."

— *Grandma Bess and Grandpa Richard*

"When I was a little girl, I would often wake up in the middle of the night. I'd wander into my mom and dad's bedroom, crawl into bed between them, and snuggle up for the rest of the night. When I was eight years old, my mom was expecting a baby. One night, like many other nights, I crept into my parent's bedroom, slipped into bed beside my mom and cuddled up. I felt an arm circle round me and draw me close, and I started to drift off to sleep. A voice spoke soft words to me, but the voice startled me. It wasn't my mom! I cried out, jumped out of bed and ran to the bathroom to hide. A moment later, I heard the soft shuffle of slippers, and the door of the bathroom slowly opened. There was my grandmother's round face peeking at me; I could see the curlers in her hair. She was grinning. She spread her arms open wide and said, 'She's here! You have a baby sister!' I squealed and ran to her. My grandmother hugged me and, though it was the middle of the night, allowed me to ask endless questions about babies, where they come from, and when I could see my baby sister. She never got angry that I didn't recognize her voice—she never even mentioned it. She just patiently answered my questions in a way that soothed an excited eight-year-old back to sleep." — *Karen*

Grandparents are a continuing legacy...

...a connection to your family history. Ask your grandparents to help you create a family tree; for locked in their memories may be the names and birth dates of ancestors in your past.

*Uncles and aunts and cousins, are all very well, and
fathers and mothers are not to be despised; but a
grandmother at holiday time is worth them all.*

FANNY FERN

Circle of Life

Kids can say the funniest things when they're talking to or about their grandparents. My grandson once asked me why my skin was so squishy. And here I am thinking I'm in great shape for my age! On the other hand, he likes the fact that I can ski and kayak—and those are things we can now do together. Though I am the very last to learn about the newest smartphone apps, my granddaughters are happy to show me what to do, and I'm delighted to learn something new from them!

Often, your grandparents were the ones who taught you a new skill, like fishing, or knitting, or woodcarving. In some cases, they were the folks who raised you, and helped instill your moral compass and real life values.

Clearly, different generations have different ways of expressing themselves through music, art, speech, and the written word. And while it's true that vernacular changes between generations can be as confusing as if we're speaking different languages, what doesn't get lost in translation is the deep attachment, care, and love that flows between us.

Grandparents and grandkids have a great deal they can share with one another—humor, wisdom, skills, and compassion—and all of these are clearly understood, whether we speak the same language or not!

Learn to appreciate the wisdom gained by a lifetime of experiences.

"To know who you are, you have to know where you came from. On my family's side, time and circumstance prevented me from knowing my grandparents, except for wisps of memory as a young child. But I have been able to have a sense of my context in the world through my wife's mother, the grandmother to my children. Her story of making it out of the bleak, depressed mining town of Butte, Montana, and having made it by hardscrabble work and determination to the mild climes and gentle world of Montecito, allows my children to understand that what we have is not a right or an inevitability, but a gift to be hard won and appreciated. And there is nothing sweeter than the steady flowing of the unconditional love of the grandmother, nurturing my children in a non-judgmental embrace that from her position of years and experience, gives them grounding and context in their own lives, an incalculable gift that will last their lifetimes until they, too, are able to pass it on." — *Paul*

The dawn is not distant, nor is the
night starless; love is eternal
HENRY WADSWORTH LONGFELLOW

"Having a grandparent in your life should mean more than annual birthday cards and someone who comes along to your graduation. The stories and history they hold is extraordinary and beautiful, once you take the time to invest in it. If you have a weekend to spend with them, take it. If they live far away, set aside an hour of your night to call them. They won't be around forever, so make sure they know how much you love them." — *Lauren*

" 'You are so much like your grandmother…you have her kindness and grace.' These are words to live up to, especially since I never met either my grandmother or my grandfather. My grandmother died at Auschwitz. My grandfather died at Buchenwald. When you meet your grandparents through the memories of others, they are still a cherished part of your life. Perhaps you appreciate them even more. I will always strive for kindness and grace with my grandchildren, and all children that come into and pass through my life, so I can truly be like my grandmother." — *June*

"I have distinct memories of my Nana—my mom's mom. I know I was lucky to have been able to spend time with her. She was a diminutive lady of Norwegian and Swedish descent. She may have been tiny, but that didn't stop her from being quietly strong. She raised five children—much of that time as a widow. Her husband—my mom's dad, passed away when my mother was just 18, and mom was the eldest of the five kids.

When I visited my Nana, her house was like a treasure chest. The photos and her china, the aroma from her kitchen, and even the ticking of her clock were interesting to me. She'd break the rules and let me drink coffee, even before I was old enough. And she taught me how to knit—a skill that I utilize and cherish to this day. If I ever felt blue or had a tummyache, she'd serve me milk toast—a simple, soothing recipe that had been passed to her from her own Scandinavian grandparents. When I remember my Nana, I see her smiling face. Her eyes are crinkled into little almond-shapes, and have nearly disappeared behind her round glasses. This is the face she always showed me. Even when her arms were wrapped around me, and I couldn't see her face, I knew she was smiling. I could just feel it." — *Candace*

A single conversation across the table
with a wise man is better than ten
years mere study of books

HENRY WADSWORTH LONGFELLOW

"Grandma and Grandpa, you have always been a blessing in my life—giving me strength and courage not only through the best of times but the most difficult as well. You've stood by my side and your encouragement has helped me persevere. Thank you for your wisdom, courage, compassion, and for your unconditional love. Some of my most treasured memories are of the road trips we took when I was younger. I loved sitting in the back of the truck, gazing out the window at the countryside and listening to your stories about how the mountains and rocks were formed all around us. Every new town we visited became an adventure, and grandma and I would buy postcards to document this in an album we were creating. At the end of each day, I'd look forward to the 'bag house' that we would stay in. This was a phrase I created as an alternative to 'motel', because whenever we stopped for the night, we would bring our bags of clothes with us. I'll never forget how much you both laughed when I first said this and it became our private joke for many years after." — *Ashley*

"My paternal grandmother lived the longest of my grandparents, and was very near and dear to my heart. She passed away the day before I gave birth to my second child, my daughter. It was as though two souls passed in the heavens, sharing a moment before making their separate entrances. Such is the circle that brings us all together, as my father went to her funeral with pictures of his granddaughter in hand. A celebration of life, love, and the family that binds us together." — *Eleanor V.*

"Grandparents are noble teachers. My grandfather taught me to fish and to love the sea. What began as joyful moments with a man I loved has become my livelihood. Now I am teaching my grandson, so that he will not only be able to provide for his family one day, but also so he can understand the simple pleasure of spending time with those you love." — *Rich*

If nothing is going well,
call your grandmother

ITALIAN PROVERB

"Time spent with your grandparents is a funny thing and often not appreciated until those moments are long gone. Afterwards you realize how formative the accumulation of all those moments were on your life. Those moments for me always include the many camping trips with my grandparents. The trips fostered in me the appreciation of the simple pleasures in life: eating Tootsie Rolls with my grandma around a campfire, walking with my grandpa to buy the firewood for the fire later that night, and playing beauty shop with my sisters in the middle of that motor home. But, most importantly, learning that the lasting, simple pleasures in life are not tangible items I can hold or see, but the feelings and memories that I hold in my heart, and the thankfulness to my grandparents for showing them to me." — *Amanda*

"My grandma loved to have us over for gatherings for our birthdays and the holidays. She would tell us to 'share our love—do not keep it all to yourself.' My grandma spread love like melted butter on her hot homemade bread." — *Jerome*

And finally...letting go

Ever has it been that love knows not its own depth
until the hour of separation

KHALIL GIBRAN

The circle of life is a natural phenomenon, and a mystery. We see it playing out in nature every day; in the turning of the seasons; from summer to fall, from winter to spring. We study seasonal changes in school, and are enthralled by the beauty of plants, trees and flowers as the life cycle begins, grows, ends, and begins again. The dramatic spectacle that Mother Nature provides, and the obvious symbiotic relationship between all living things is fascinating; a wonder to behold. But it is also full of mystery, because it is utterly beyond our control.

As humans, we are all a part of this master plan, and our life cycle also has a beginning, a middle, and, at some point, an end. Though we may understand intellectually that once a human is born the clock begins to tick, in actuality letting go of our loved ones is a difficult subject to contemplate, let alone endure.

You may count yourself among the very lucky if you have been blessed to enjoy the love, wisdom, and companionship of your grandparents into the twilight of their lives. The love you have for them never leaves you. The memories are yours to keep forever. Treasure them. Share their stories with your children and family members. In this way, you can continue to build on the circle of which you are a part. The love you shared with your beloved grandparents will be an imprint that you will always carry with you—and in due course, will pass along to others.

Picture Credits

ph = photographer

Page 1 Arendal Keramik (www.arendal-ceramics.com), ph: Debi Treloar Page 2 © i love images / gardening / Alamy Page 4 The home of Vidar and Ingrid Aune Westrum, ph: Debi Treloar Page 5 The home of Ida Susanne Collier of sukkertoyforoyet.blogspot.no, ph: Catherine Gratwicke Page 6 insert The home of Vidar and Ingrid Aune Westrum, ph: Debi Treloar Page 8 © Christine Mariner / Design Pics/Getty Images Page 9 ph: Polly Wreford Page 10 ph: Carolyn Barber Page 13 The family home of Lea Bawnager, Vayu Robins & Elliot Bawnager-Robins, owner of affär, ph: Debi Treloar Page 14 ph: Polly Wreford Page 15 The home of Anne Bjelke hapelbloggen.blogspot.no, ph: Catherine Gratwicke Page 17 ph: Dan Duchars Page 18 Troels Graugaard/Getty Images Page 20 ph: Kate Whitaker Page 21 Arendal Keramik (www.arendal-ceramics.com), ph: Debi Treloar Page 22 ph: Polly Wreford Page 25 The family home in Norfolk of Laura & Fred Ingrams of Arie & Ingrams Design, ph: Debi Treloar Page 26 Mark Bowden/Getty Images Page 27 ph: Claire Richardson Page 28–29 ph: Paul Massey Page 30 Home of Tim Rundle

and Glynn Jones, ph: Debi Treloar Page 33 Bed of Flowers, B&B owned by Floriene Bosch www.bedofflowers.nl, ph: Debi Treloar Page 34 The home of artist Claire Basler in France, ph: Debi Treloar Page 35 The home of the artist Lou Kenlock, Oxfordshire, ph: Catherine Gratwicke Page 37 The home of Inger Lill Skagen in Norway, ph: Debi Treloar Page 38 Westend61/Getty Images Page 41 ph: Kate Whitaker Page 42 Yuri Arcurs / Alamy Page 43 ph: Polly Wreford Page 45 The Family home of Shella Anderson, Tollesbury, UK, ph: Debi Treloar Page 46 & 48 ph: Polly Wreford Page 49 ph: Carolyn Barber Page 50 The family home in Norfolk of Laura & Fred Ingrams of Arie & Ingrams Design, ph: Debi Treloar Page 51 The Norfolk family home of the designer Petra Boase, ph: Debi Treloar Page 53 The Family home of Shella Anderson, Tollesbury, UK, ph: Debi Treloar Page 54 The Barton's seaside home in West Sussex: thedodo.co.uk, ph: Paul Massey Page 55, ph: Ian Wallace Page 57 Fuse/Getty Images Page 58 The London home of stylist Selina Lake (selinalake.blogspot.com), ph: Debi Treloar Page 61 The home of Vidar and Ingrid Aune Westrum, ph: Debi Treloar Page 63 ph: Carolyn Barber

Grandparents are similar to a piece of string—
handy to have around and easily wrapped
around the fingers of their grandchildren.

AUTHOR UNKNOWN

*Grandparents are similar to a piece of string—
handy to have around and easily wrapped
around the fingers of their grandchildren.*

AUTHOR UNKNOWN

Acknowledgments

First and foremost, I lovingly dedicate this book to my grandmothers Nellie and Olga—'Granny' and 'Nana' to me. They introduced me to canning and needlework; skills that enrich my life. And to my Grandpa, who lived to the mighty age of 94. He was blind in his later years, but back in his heyday he would create stop-action animated films for my brother, sister, cousins, and me to show where he and Granny had been on their road trips. For an old-fashioned guy, he was quite advanced!

I also want to acknowledge my own sweet mother and dear dad. They have been wonderful grandparents to my children, and now they've been able to watch me become a grandmother and are happily cherishing four great-grandchildren as well.

Two more Grandmothers were a part of our family, and near and dear to my heart. Gramma She She, my son-in-law's mother, passed away at a young age, but she was able to have time with the grandchildren we share, which was a blessing for us all. And lastly, there is Nona, the matriarch of our family—my husband's mom, Virginia. She lived a very long life—she was 102 when she passed away. She was the grandest of all grandmothers, and she left us with a treasure chest of rich cultural traditions, colloquialisms, recipes, and rules to live by. Through her example, we learned to be strong but kind, to have humor and courage, and to always see the positive in life. We'll cherish our memories of her, always.